Pow

MW00938509

Beginner to Pro Guide

By

Timothy Short

Introduction

I wish to thank you and congratulate you for purchasing the book, *"Powershell: Beginner to Pro Guide.*

This book contains proven steps and strategies on how to learn the processes and strategies behind programming and scripting with Powershell (PS).

You will first learn exactly what PS is and the benefits of using it over other scripting languages. You will also learn the terminology used when using PS.

On top of this you will also learn all of the core aspects of Programming with PS, including the use of cmdlets (commands).

As you progress through this book, you will learn how to use a variety of illustrations, as well as variables (scalers), operators (oper.), and wildcards.

By the time you complete this book you will know what PowerShell is and go as far as creating and utilizing your own drives!

Thanks again for choosing this book, I hope you enjoy it!

© **Copyright 2016 by DCB Web Trading Ltd_____ - All rights reserved.**

This document is geared towards providing exact and reliable information in regards to the topic and issue covered. The publication is sold with the idea that the publisher is not required to render accounting, officially permitted, or otherwise, qualified services. If advice is necessary, legal, or professional, a practiced individual in the profession should be ordered.

- From a Declaration of Principles which was accepted and approved equally by a Committee of the American Bar Association and a Committee of Publishers and Associations.

In no way is it legal to reproduce, duplicate, or transmit any part of this document in either electronic means or in printed format. Recording of this publication is strictly prohibited and any storage of this document is not allowed unless with written permission from the publisher. All rights reserved.

The information provided herein is stated to be truthful and consistent, in that any liability, in terms of inattention or otherwise, by any usage or abuse of any policies, processes, or directions contained within is the solitary and utter responsibility of the recipient reader. Under no circumstances will any legal responsibility or blame be held against the publisher for any reparation, damages, or monetary loss due to the information herein, either directly or indirectly.

Respective authors own all copyrights not held by the publisher.

The information herein is offered for informational purposes solely, and is universal as so. The presentation of the information is without contract or any type of guarantee assurance.

The trademarks that are used are without any consent, and the publication of the trademark is without permission or backing by the trademark owner. All trademarks and brands within this book are for clarifying purposes only and are the owned by the owners themselves, not affiliated with this document.

Table of Contents

7

Chapter 1: Learning a New Language

It is paramount to acknowledge while going through this guide that you are learning a new language. If you have ever attempted to learn a new language before, you know that it is not anything, which can be achieved in one sitting. To learn a new language will take time and effort, however learning to speak computer is arguably a lot easier than learning to speak a new tongue. Just thinking about learning "scripting" may seem daunting, but it is not hard at all to learn. Scripting is nothing more than writing instructions in a manner that a computer can understand so that the computer will do the things that you need it to do.

Now, there are more than 6,000 spoken languages in today's world. Each has its own way to speak or spell words, and these spellings can shift and change within the same language. These subtle changes, even in the English language, cause inconsistencies and make learning such a language very difficult. PS, on the other hand, does not have those kinds of incongruencies, so it is simpler to grasp the concepts and to put into practice. You might be familiar with the traditional command shells used by Windows, like cmd.exe. PS is much more flexible and much more powerful than that.

The following chapters will help to guide you in getting started in speaking PS, allowing you to utilize this wonderful resource. The material in this manual will help you whether you are brand new to programming, an intermediate user looking to get back to the basics, or a veteran programmer checking out PS for the first time.

In Chapter 2, we will go over commands and your first, basic PS commands. Additionally, we will inform you the steps to utilize the built-in help tutorial for any issues that you run into in the future.

In Chapter 3, we will demonstrate the commands that transfers objects from one series to another; using this command as a pipeline. When you utilize a string of commands in order to transfer down a line of commands, you initiate PS commands or illustrations. You will learn how to sort and format such illustrations. With these illustrations, you will find that you can complete much more complex tasks.

In Chapter 4, we will introduce you to the wildcards and oper.s that you will commonly use in PS. These will equip you with a way to create expressions within illustrations, allowing more functionality and even further complex actions to be completed.

In Chapter 5, you will discover how to handle the strings within commands. You will learn such things as when you need to use double or single quotes to enclose strings. Additionally, you will learn how and when to flag or escape, characters embedded in such strings.

In Chapter 6, we will go over scalers. These are basically virtual boxes that are used as virtual storage for you to transfer and store data using PS code. You can fill these boxes, or duffel bags, yourself for user defined scalers, or you can use pre-packaged versions with built-in scalers.

In Chapter 7, we will go over PS providers, as well as built-in drives. You will learn what providers are and what they do, as well as drives that you can access and what procedure you need to follow to successfully use them.

We suggest that you practice with each chapter of instructions because in practicing you will become accomplished. Reading the material gives you knowledge but practice will imprint the instructions into your memory. Doing so will provide you with direct, first-hand knowledge and visual indications on exactly how each topic we cover works. It is far more difficult to learn a language without practice!

Chapter 2: Beginning to Work With PS

By this time, you, as well as most administrators, have probably become at least basically familiar with PS. Maybe you have downloaded it, fiddled with it a bit, and maybe you have ever used it in order to perform basic functions, like ad hoc tasks, that you might have done with a typical command shell, or cmd.exe. PS, however, is much more advanced than a DOS style command shell. PS is a command-line scripting environment that utilizes the Microsoft .Net CLR, or Common Language Runtime, and the .NET framework. You are employing .NET objects when you are operating in the PS environment.

The services that you access or the folder systems that you view are really just instances of objects. These objects represent the services and the folders, whereas other command shells simply process the text. Because of this, PS gives you far more function and potential than previous command shells. These lessons will inform you of the way to utilize this power in order to perform assorted exercises.

For a beginner, it is paramount not to skip ahead, as each chapter in this book builds upon the last. This is done so as to demonstrate the paramount PS concepts. In this chapter, we will cover how to go down the path of using PS. We will also cover basic commands you will come across while using this new language. Finally, at the conclusion of this section, we will discuss the ways you can resource a help function while inside of PS while creating commands, strings, pipelines, and illustrations, as well as when it is appropriate to use aliases.

Getting Started with PS

There are various different locales for which you can download PS. Do not download from any doubtful source; only download from providers that you trust. Before the downloading of PS, you must have already installed the .NET Framework 2.0. When this task has been accomplished, the installation process is rather quick and straightforward. Be careful, though, you need to make a positive confirmation that you are specifically installing the PS edition that has been created for your operating system. There are editions available for Windows 2003, Windows XP service pack 2, Server 2008 beta 3,and Windows Vista. We are running on Windows XP.

Once the installation of PS is complete, it is ready for use. To run PS, you will first go to your Start menu, then "All Programs", and choose "Windows PS 1.0", and then click "Windows Power-Shell". Once the PS window loads up, you will see a command prompt displaying the current folder from which you are operating. Now you are ready to begin writing and executing commands with PS.

Commands

As we have discussed before, PS uses its own scripting language, based upon the .NET framework. The foundational command, which is the most basic, is the command, which you would pronounce as command-let. A command performs a specific task, like retrieving the contents of a folder or updating an entry to a registry, which makes it very similar to a function. There are more than 100 commands built into PS. Additionally, you can create your own commands, but it is a necessary requirement that it is in a computer language, a .NET language, that can be recognized, like C# or Visual Basic .NET. In this book, we will only be discussing the built-in commands.

For a more consistent naming convention, each command is written in the verb-noun form. This makes PS consistent, easy to learn, and easy to expand. The verb is the action word part of the command and the noun defines upon where the action will be performed. In order to run the command, you will type the requirements into the PS command prompt and then press Enter. The outcomes of the command will be shown beneath the command prompt. That is how you run a basic command in PS.

There will be times that your memory escapes you; you will wish to know if there is already a command for that which you wish to accomplish, or maybe a wisp of a memory is there and you know what you think you know, but can't really reach to grab hold. No worries! You can type the **Get-Command** and it will give a comprehensive list of commands. You now possess the secret list, alas; it does not come with a description. For a description, you must now access the **Get-Help** command.

Command Help

Within PS there is an accessible sequence of Help files for you to use whenever necessary. From the PS command window using the previously mentioned **Get-Help** command, choose **Get-Help** in conjunction with the parameter specific to the task, follow this with a command for which you need advice. Similar to the parameters used in cmd.exe commands, PS commands' parameters are used to provide specifics that the commands require to perform their task. In cmd.exe commands, these parameters would either start with a slash, a hyphen, or nothing at all. The parameters for PS commands, on the other hand, will always begin with a hyphen. Again, PS is designed to be consistent. Now, let's try something specific with using the help command.

A common task that system administrator might come across could be reading text files. After using **Get-Command** to view a complete list of available commands, you might think **Get-Contet** is where you should go, but you are not entirely certain. So let's be sure. In order to get information on GetContent, you will enter the syntax **Get-Help -name Get-Content**. This will return the command description and the syntax information. You will also see that this command, **Get-Content**, is used in order to return the contents of an item, or any type of file on the system.

You may have previously used the For command in a WSH, or Windows Script Host, for batch files or File- SystemObject object. For PS, this task is accomplished with the simple **Get-Content** command. You can access particularized information regarding the syntax by simply inserting the **-full** extension to the request, like this: **Get-Help -name[space]Get-Content -full**. You should notice the **-full** extension does not take on a comparable value. In this instance, this specific parameter is known as a "switch parameter." It is identified so as it switches the action of the command. After running this command, it might be best to resize or scroll in order to locate the PARAMETERS category. This category gives you the information needed to add parameter extensions to the command. There are two relevant categories for these specific parameters. They are the terms Required and/or Position.

As expected, the Required category indicates if the parameter is optional or mandatory. If Required is set at true, then you are required to include the parameter. If Required is set to false, then it is optional.

Position indicates if the parameter requires a name or if it should be referenced from position. If Position is placed at "named," you are required to include the name of the extension parameter when referencing it. If Position is set to number, you have a choice to either reference the parameter with a name or simply provide the value in the corresponding position.

For example, the **-path** parameter is a requisite when using the **Get-Content** command. In this illustration, you can add the parameter value in the front position without providing the name of the parameter, like this: **Get-Content c:\sample.txt** A paramount reminder: If a parameter value has spaces in it, you must enclose that value in quotes.

More information in the PARAMETERS section includes the determinate data the parameter value must include. This information is after the parameter and angle brackets (<>). For example, **-path** parameter value is required to qualify as a string. Now, if there is a couplet of brackets, or [ ], that follows the word string, then the parameter value is permitted to be a string array.

Switch parameters don't have values. For such parameters, data type is sufficient. To show an illustration: **Get-Content's -forced** parameter is determined with this type of data. It invalidates restrictions that would, otherwise, obstruct the cmd

17

from completion. This override only occurs when the parameter is included in the command.

Another extremely useful feature included in PShell is parameter name completion. To initiate this course of action, you just have to enter enough of the parameter name to differentiate it from the others. Here is an example: **Get-Content c:\sample.txt -force** is the same command as **Get-Content c:\sample.txt -fo**

Along with providing parameter information for building commands, the help file in **Get-Content** also includes examples the proper use of the command, great tips included in the Notes section, as well as where to locate additional information. Remember, there are help files for every command, as well as for the more general concepts.

The Help file gives the parameter specifics you need for building commands. Get-Content Help file explains how the command works, includes helpful tips, suggests resources for extra notes and information. Help files are everywhere for every part of PS. commands are all included in Help, plus general knowledge. Make a point of surfing the Help file and operating through each command one by one. If will familiarize you with commands and codes and build your confidence.

Concepts Help

If you are looking for an overview of a variety of concepts within PS, there is a set of help files included to do just that. Each of these files begins with **about_** and ends with the topic

name. To look at the complete listing of topics, alphabetically, enter the command: **Get-Help about***
If you already know the topic that you need an overview of, simply include the full name of the topic as a parameter value. If you wished to return a file concerning flow control, then enter this command: **Get-Help about_fow_control** This is a helpful tool to utilize when wishing or needing more information regarding commands, at your disposal.

Aliases

There are some commands with names that are very wordy. If you have to continually retype them, it can get pretty annoying. Lucky for us, then, that PS allows us to use aliases in order to refer to commands. An alias, as you would expect, is an alternate name that is a lot shorter than the original. Consider it a shortcut or a nickname for your command. Much like commands themselves, PS has many built-in aliases. And, again, like the commands, you can invent and embed your particular aliases. In order to look at the aliases available to you while in your session, enter the: **Get-Alias command**

Now, just for clarification, your current session refers specifically to your current connection to PS. When you first start PS, you are creating a new session. That session will remain until you x closed and exit PS, which then, ends the connection and the session. On top of displaying built in aliases and linked commands, **Get-Alias** also displays user created aliases that were created during that session, as well as aliases that are defined in the profiles, user configurations that are pre-loaded into PS on startup.

If you need to view a specified command's aliases, you must first identify the specific **Get- Alias** command. For an illustration, if you are desiring to view the aliases that are available for the command **Get-ChildItem**, then you need to enter this command:

Get-Alias |
Where-Object {$_.definition `
-match "Get-ChildItem"}

There are a few elements in this command that you may not yet understand. We will be going over that information later in the book. However, what is paramount to learn for now is that the outcome of the **Get-Alias** command is directed to a **Where-Object** command in order to filter out results that do not match the **Get-ChildItem.** In order to search for different aliases, simply replace **Get-ChildItem** with the subsequent command name. PS utilizes three different aliases that refer to **Get-ChildItem** and these are gci, ls, and dir. Each of these will offer the same result, as follows:

Get-ChildItem c:\windows
dir c:\windows
ls c:\windows
gci c:\windows

The four above commands will all return information on the C:\Windows folder's contents.

If you choose to create your own alias within a current session, you could use the **Set-Alias** command. It's really very easy. Let us say you are wishing to create an alias for **Get-Content** and you wish to name it **cnt**, you could run the following command:

Set-Alias cnt Get-Content

Now that you have created this new alias, you can use **cnt** anywhere you would typically use **Get-Content**, and that alias will stay active until you end the current PS session or close PS. acknowledge you can't include parameters while you are characterizing an alias, you can only include the command name. If you are wishing to define a reference to the command and parameters, then you should probably generate a function.

Chapter Summary

So far you have learned the beginning of PS command usage. You should now be familiar with what a command is, how to locate and access help files, how to locate and use an alias, as well as how to design and use an alias of your own. As you continue to learn PS programming from this book, you will gain additional knowledge on how to use commands and how fully to utilize PS to its wonderful potential. Until that time, we highly recommend that you seize a time to practice what you have realized in this chapter. In order to reap the full benefits of the guide, you should practice as you go through each chapter to compound and solidify your knowledge. Use the help files to practice and try out different parameters with your commands.

Chapter 3: Pipelines and Outputs

So far you have learned what commands are and the rudiments of running commands. You have also learned how to do some research using the Help files in order to figure out exactly what each command does. Additionally, you have learned how to create and utilize aliases in order to customize your experience. On top of all of this, you have learned how parameters work, how to use them properly, and the data types that they require, allowing you to utilize an even wider variety of commands.

As powerful as commands are by themselves, it might not be quite enough to provide one with the outcomes that you desire. It is because of this that PS lets you create pipelines. These link commands in order to accomplish much more complex tasks, as well as refining the information that is returned to you. In this chapter, we will teach you how to link your commands into a pipeline in the creation of illustrations. In addition to this, we will also teach you how to sort and format the output of your illustrations.

As previously stated, the PS pipeline is nothing more than sets of commands which pass objects starting with one command then onto the next. Each one of those commands creates an object and sends it down the line, where the subsequent command picks it up. The command that picks it up utilizes it as an input and then generates a new output, and then sends it to the ensuing command, continuing the process until the conclusion. Commands are connected into a pipeline via the utilization of the pipe oper. (|).

In traditional command shells, the results from a pipeline are all returned at once. That means that all results from the entire pipeline are returned as an entire single result set. PS is different in this regard as well. The results are sent across the pipeline and as soon as one command returns the result it is instantly accessible to the next command in that pipeline.

For instance, in the event that you utilize the command **Get-Service,** you will then get a rundown of all services at currently introduced on your framework. At the point when this is done, you will see that the command gives back the name, status, and display of every administration on your system.

Now, let's say that instead of returning an entire rundown of services on your system that you instead need to return that list of the services that are currently running. To fulfill this you can make a pipeline from **Get-Service** to **Where-Object** commands. You will send the result of **Get-Service** to **Where-Object**, which will filter the output based on criteria you specified, like this:

Get-Service | Where-Object {$_.status -eq 'running'}

Observe the use of the pipeline oper. (|), which is connecting the commands. As you have already seen, the **Get-Service** command produces an object containing a full list of service-related information. By using the pipeline oper, the object is then sent to the **Where-Object** command as an input. **Where-Object** is then used to filter information based upon Status property value expression, which you will notice is in braces ({ }). If that expression is then evaluated as true, the object is sent along the pipeline filtering out any objects or information that does not meet the criteria.

In this example, the **-eq** oper. within the expression is used to state that the Status property has to equal the **'running'** string. Remember, you can see all available properties with the Help files. Status is a property that is available to an object that you generate with the **Get-Service** command. By passing the object along the pipeline you can access the properties of the object, like we did using **Where-Object**. In order to do this, you can utilize the **$_** scaler. This scaler will hold the object each time **Where-Object** gets looped through pipeline results. This allows reference the properties of the object, like we did with **$_.Status**.

Say you wish to limit returned information even more, and you only wish the display name information to be returned. You can then send output of **Where-Object** to a **Select-Object** command, as follows:

Get-Service |
 where {$_.status -eq 'running'} |
select displayname

For the previous illustration, the object gets received by **Select-Object** from the **Where-Object** command. The illustration then utilizes **where** alias in order to reference **Where-Object** and **select** alias in order to reference **Select-Object**. For **select**, we specified the property name that we wished to display, which we specified as **displayname**. When the information is returned, you will see that the data has been filtered according to specifications.

When employing pipelines it's paramount that you remember you are operating with objects. Each individual command will make an object that gets received by the next. The final command also generates an object, which outputs the illustration results. Moving deeper into chapter 3, we teach you to use the output objects and properties in order to further refine your illustrations in PS.

Format Output

PS is defaulted to automatically format illustrations based on the data type in the output.

Get-Process PS

This illustration is used to return data on the PS process. This will display the output of the command. If you wish something different from default output format, you can utilize a pipeline using one of the four supported format output commands that PS supports. Here are those four commands:

1. **Format-Table**: This command displays the returned data in a table, which is default for the majority of commands. Because of this you typically won't need to specify this output.
2. **Format-List:** This will return data in list form.
3. **Format-Wide:** This command will return the data via wide table format. This table will include just one value for each item displayed.
4. **Format-Custom:** This command will return the data via custom format, which will be based upon saved configuration data. This is in a .ps1xml file format. If you wish to update this, use **Update-Format- Data**.

Here is a formatting example of the last PS process illustration:

Get-Process PS |
 Format-List

It is paramount to know that different formats may return different information. Some formats include more detailed information than others. In this case, the original table format had more information displayed then the new list format.

PS will determine how to format results based upon the type of object. This type of format, the layout, and the properties that are you get are tied to the object type. For instance, the data retrieved by **Get-ChildItem** is different when returning information on file systems versus when it is retrieving information on registries. This is because these are different kinds of objects even being that they are accessed with the same illustration. A complex set of XML format (.ps1xml) files is used in order for PS to determine exactly how to display such results.

Control Output

Unless overridden, PS will apply the default output format and send it to the output console window whenever an illustration is executed. This override can be performed using any one of the four formatting commands mentioned previously. In addition to this, it is also possible to control where that output is sent. This can be done via the use of the following commands:

1. **Out-Host:** This command is the default and does not need specification. It sends the output to your console.
2. **Out-Default:** This doesn't need to be specified either. It sends the output to whatever the default formatting command may be. It also delegates out process to **Out-Host**.
3. **Out-File**: This command directs the output to a chosen file.
4. **Out-Null:** This command deletes the output. Nothing is returned to the PS console.
5. **Out-Printer:** This command will direct the output to a specified printer.
6. **Out-String:** This command will convert the object to a string array.

Remember the help files if you need further assistance with these commands.

To properly use the above commands, they will be added to the pipeline's end. Continuing with the previous example, we will put the PS process information into the format of a list. That list will then be sent to the file:

Get-Process PS |
 Format-List |
 Out-File C:\SysInfo\ps.txt

When directing and output to a file, PS will not display it in the console. It will only save the contents to the specified file. You wish to be sure to only send the output to files that make sense. You don't wish to send a text to a .bmp file, for example. Doing so would not produce an error, but you would not be capable of viewing the output when you attempt to open the file. In addition to directing the output to a file, the **Out- File** will allow you to choose to append or replace existing content with current output. If not directed to do so otherwise, PS replaces any existing content. It does so by default. In order to append output to file, you will need to add an **-append** switch at the end of the **Out-File** command, as follows:

Get-Process PS |
Format-List |
Out-File C:\SysInfo\ps.txt `
-append

Sort Output

The formatting output is very helpful, but you will likely wish to sort the output as well. To do this, we will utilize **Sort-Object**. This command will take the input objects of the pipeline and sort them based on criteria that we define. As you have already learned, PS will stream results along pipelines, one command to the next one in line. When sorting data, however, the **Sort-Object** command will wait until all objects or results have been retrieved, and then it will sort them. This basically stops the fluid streaming process until the sorting is complete. This is not an issue for small returns, but it can drastically impact performance when retrieving much larger quantities of data. Do not let this dissuade use of this command in its entirety, though, as the **Sort-Object** can still be very useful. For instance, let's say we wish a list of items from the C:\Windows folder. To accomplish this, we can utilize the **Get-ChildItem** command like this:

```
dir c:\windows |
where {$_.length -gt 500000} |
sort -property length
-descending
```

Here is what happens. The command passes the object from **Get-ChildItem**, which we utilized its **dir** alias, for **Where-Object**, for which we utilized its **where** alias. In the **Where-Object** command, we specified, by utilizing **-gt,** length will be greater than 500,000 bytes. The object is then sent along the pipeline to **Sort-Object**. Once the **Sort-Object** command, for which we utilized **sort**, has retrieved all the objects, it then organizes based upon the criteria that we specified.

In this example, we had the **Sort-Object** command was used to first sort the data based on its length, via **-property length.** We then utilized the **-descending** switch in order to show that the data should be returned in descending order. If the **-descending** switch is not specified, then the results will be returned in ascending order. It is also possible to specify additional properties to be sorted by separating them with commas. PS will sort data in the order of property appearance.

Chapter Summary

You learned in this chapter just how powerful the pipelines in PS can be, and how to combine multiple commands in order to perform multiple successive operations on objects. In addition to building a pipeline, you have also learned how to format the output of the pipeline, where you can send that output information to, as well as multiple ways to sort that information. In the following chapters, you will learn how to further refine your illustrations so that you can more fully utilize the benefits of pipelines. Before moving forward, it is a good idea to take what you have learned in this chapter and practice. Once you are comfortable with the knowledge you have already accessed, move ahead.

Chapter 4: Operations and Wildcards

As you have already learned, you are capable create a pipeline by connecting multiple commands, and then you can utilize the **Where-Object** command in order to filter objects that are passed along your pipeline. Look at the following illustration:

dir c:\windows |
where {$_.length -gt 500000}

In this illustration, we used the alias **dir** for the **Get-ChildItem** command and the alias **where** for the **Where-Object** command. Objects from the **Get-ChildItem** command are sent down the line to the **Where-Object** command, which then filters out all objects from the C:\Windows file that are less than 500,000 bytes.

The expression that is enclosed in braces, **{$_.length -gt 500000},** is used in order to indicate that the length property of anything returned must be greater than 500,000 bytes. The **$_.length** is utilized in order to retrieve the value of the length property. The **$_** symbol is used to reference the current pipeline object, and the **.length** is used to retrieve the length property value. Then the expression utilizes the **-gt**, or greater than, oper. in order to compare that value of length property to the target value of 500,000 bytes.

Just like with other programing languages, PS provides you with a set of oper.s. The oper's allow you to create expressions that can be utilized within your illustrations. An expression is nothing more than a block of code that PS recognizes and evaluates.

The resulting evaluation is used to determine the action that is taken. In the previous illustration, PS had to determine whether the **Where-Object** expression held to be true or false. If the expression evaluates to be true, which mean that an object meets the specified criteria, the object will then be passed down the pipeline as an output. However, if the information solves as false, which means the object does not meet the specified criteria, then the object is discarded and removed from the resulting output.

There are a variety of oper.s that are included in PS that can be utilized within expressions. In this chapter, we will discuss a variety of these oper.s as well as how to properly use them. We will also discuss how to find the properties of a command

Operators: Comparison

As you can surely deduce, these comparison oper.s are used in order to compare values. In the instances where a comparison is contained within an expression, PS will compare the values of the left to the right of the oper. The previous example utilized a comparison oper., in where the length property value was compared to 500,000 bytes. Here is a list of many of the comparison oper.s available in PS:

Operator	Description	Case-sensitive	Explicit case-insensitive
-eq	Equal to	-ceq	-ieq

-ne	Not equal to	-cne	-ine
-gt	Greater than	-cgt	-igt
-ge	Greater than or equal to	-cge	-ige
-lt	Less than	-clt	-ilt
-le	Less than or equal to	-cle	-ile
-like	Uses wildcards to find matching patterns	-clike	-ilike
-notlike	Uses wildcards to find nonmatching patterns	-cnotlike	-inotlike
-match	Uses regular expressions to find matching patterns	-cmatch	-imatch
-notmatch	Uses regular expressions to find nonmatching patterns	-cnotmatch	-inotmatch
-contains	Determines whether value on the left side of the	-ccontains	-icontains

	oper. contains the value on the right		
-notcontains	Determines whether value on the left side of the oper. does not contain the value on the right	-cnotcontains	-inotcontains
-replace	Replaces part or all of the value on left side of the oper.	-creplace	-ireplace

Let's go back to our previous example and do the opposite. In this instance, we are going to return data that is less than 500,000 bytes using the following illustration:

dir c:\windows |
where {$_.length -lt 500000}

It is apparent that the only difference between this illustration and the one that preceded it are the comparison oper.s. Previously, we used **-gt**, or greater than. For this example, we used **-lt**, or less than.

Other comparison oper.s function the same way. For example, in the next illustration, we will use the **-eq**, or equal to, oper. to compare the **responding** property value and the string true. We do this in order to access a list of processes that are responding, as follows:

get-process |
where {$_.responding -eq 'true' }

In order for the expression of the **Where-Object** to evaluate as true, then the responding property value must also equal true. Because of this, only responding processes will be returned.

All comparison oper.s, by default, will perform case insensitive comparisons. In order for more precision in coding, it is possible to add the an i to one of the comparison oper.s, like - **ieq,** in order to state explicitly that it is to carry out case insensitive comparisons. But because this happens by default, it is not necessary.

On the other hand, if you wish for the comparison to be case sensitive, you can use the letter c at the front of the oper., like **-ceq**, for example:

'True' -eq 'true'

The previous illustration will evaluate as true because it is case insensitive by default. However,

'True' -ceq 'true'

Will evaluate as false. This is because the evaluation is case sensitive.
As your expertise with PS grows, and you are capable of retrieving types of data that are case sensitive, being capable of using an oper. With case sensitivity will be extremely beneficial.

Wildcards are yet another beneficial feature of PS. Let's say, for instance, that we are not sure of the precise name of an item while creating an expression in order to compare values. What we can do is use wildcards in the value after the oper., or the compared value. The following is a list of wildcards that are supported by PS.

Operator	Description	Example	True (match)	False (no match)
*	Matches zero or more of any character	ab*	ab, abc, about	against
?	Matches any one character	r?d	red, rid, rod	bed
[char-char]	Matches a range of sequential characters	[a-h]ug	bug, dug, hug	lug
[char...]	Matches any one character in a set of characters	[cft]ool	cool, fool, tool	pool

Wildcards are utilized via the use of **-like** and **-notlike** comparison oper.s. Another term for these operators, as well as **-replace, -match,** and **-notmatch** are also referred to as pattern matching oper.s. Let's say that we are wishing to find all of the Google related processes on our system. In order to do this, we can utilize the **-like** oper. in order to return all process that were created by companies that have a name including the string Google, as follows:

et-process |
where {$_.company -like "*google*"}

The asterisk, or *, wildcard is used to match zero or more characters. This will provide you with accurate results regardless of whether the name of the company is stored in Windows under different variations. As long as it contains "google" in the name, it will be returned.

PS also supports what are called regular expressions. These are based upon the regular expression classes that are present in the Microsoft .NET Framework. Regular Expressions are implemented via the use of the **-match** and **-notmatch** oper.s. The support from PS for these expressions happens to be rather extensive and just as extensive as could be seen in any .NET language. For more information on regular expressions, look to PS's **about_comparison_oper.s** help files, as well as the **about-regular_expression** help files.

Operators: Logical

So far in this chapter, you have learned how to properly use comparison oper.s within an expression. When using such oper.s you are creating a condition that is then evaluated to determine the action that is to be taken. There are going to be situations in which you wish to utilize expressions that contain multiple conditions, such as multiple comparisons being utilized in order to determine whether or not to take that action. In order to be capable of accomplishing multiple comparisons with just one expression, you will have to use logical oper.s in or to link the desired conditions. Logical oper.s are used to specify what logic should be used when evaluating using multiple conditions. Here is a list of PS's logical oper.s.

Operator	Description
-and	Both conditions must be true for expression to evaluate to true
-or	One or both conditions must be true for expression to evaluate to true
-not	Specified condition must be false for expression to evaluate to true
!	Specified condition must be false for expression to evaluate to true

To better understand how logical oper.s are used, look at the following example:

Get-Process |
where {($_.handles -gt 500) `
-and ($_.pm -ne 0)}

As you can see, we have two conditions in the above illustration, both of which are enclosed in parentheses. The first one, which is **($_.handles -gt 500)** is being used in order to specify that the number of handles has to be greater than, -**gt,** 500 for the process. The second one, which is **($_.pm -ne 0)**, is being used in order to specify that the paged memory, **pm**, size cannot be equal to, **-ne**, zero. Also, the **-and** logical oper. is utilized in order to connect both conditions within the expression. Both of theses conditions have to be evaluated to true for the entirety of the expression, which is enclosed in the braces **{($_.handles -gt 500) ` -and ($_.pm -ne 0)}.** Only the processes that are capable of meeting both conditions will be returned by the illustration.

Instead of using the **-and** oper., you can use the **-or** oper., as follows:

get-process |
where {($_.handles -gt 500) `
-or ($_.pm -ne 0)}

Again, the only difference between this illustration and the preceding illustration is that we are now using the **-or** oper. rather than the **-and** oper..

In this instance, it is likely that more results will return. The reason for this is that rather than having to evaluate true for both, the process only needs to evaluate true for one or both. It will only take one of the conditions to be true in order for the process to be included. In other words, for this example, the process must have either a handle count that is greater than, **-gt**, 500 or the paged memory size, **pm**, can not be equal, **-ne**, to zero, or both. This is why you will have a larger number of processes returned.

Alternately, you can utilize the **-not** logical oper. in conjunction with the **-and** oper. in order to indicate that specific criteria cannot be true, as follows:

get-process |
where {($_.handles -gt 100) `
-and -not ($_.company -eq `

"Microsoft Corporation")}

In this example, we specify that the handle count cannot be greater than 100. We also specify that the name of the company, **$_.company** cannot be **Microsoft Corporation.** This illustration will then return all non-Microsoft related processes.

Operators: Arithmetic

PS also supports oper.s that are capable of performing mathematical operations. These are called arithmetic oper.s. Here is a list of a few basic examples of arithmetic oper.s:

Operator	Description	Example	Result
+	Adds two values	10 + 5	15
-	Subtracts one value from another	10 − 5	5
-	Converts a value to a negative number	-5 + 10	5
*	Multiples two values	10 * 5	50
/	Divides two values	10 / 5	2
%	Returns the remainder from divided numbers	10 % 3	1

These oper.s can be used for more than just mathematical processes. For instance, you can use the **+** oper. in order to concatenate, or link string values, as follow:

"Use + to add two" +
" " + "strings together".

You will see further, more complex examples of the use of arithmetic oper.s as you continue through this book. This was merely an introduction to such oper.s. Don't forget about the help files, as they can provide a large amount of useful information on these oper.s, via **about_arithmetic_oper.s.**

Command Properties

There have been multiple references to different command properties so far in this book, specifically in the **Where-Object** expressions, like Handles and Length. For more information on this, you can utilize the **Get-Member** command in order to retrieve members, such as methods and properties, of commands and other objects. We went off the **Get-Command, Get-Help,** and **Get-Content** commands in chapter 2. However, you cannot use the **Get-Member** command in illustrations like **Get-Process.**

In order to be capable of accessing members using **Get-Member** you will first have to specify the object in question and then send that object down the pipeline. For instance, if you wish to have the members of the **Get-Process** command returned, you will have to type the following illustration:

Get-Process | Get-Member

This will return all members of the associated object, in this case, it is **Get-Process.** You should notice the AliasProperty entries that are listed under the MemberType category. PS not only supports regular properties, but it also supports script properties and alias properties. Much like an alias for a command, an alias property is an alternate name linked to a regular property. For example, the ProcessName property has an alias property of Name. A script property is just a property for which the output came from a script. Again, do not forget about the benefits of PS's help files. Utilize this to learn more about the **Get-Member** command.

Chapter Summary

You learned, in this chapter, about a variety of oper.s that are supported within PS, and how these oper.s allow you to create more complex expressions, as well as performing calculations. There are many more oper.s out there for you to discover, like the bitwise oper.s. Bitwise oper.s allow you to perform different binary operations and assignment operations that will assign values to different scalers. We will be going over many of these oper.s as we continue throughout the book. Before moving forward, practice what you have learned in this and previous chapters. While practicing you can utilize PS's help files in order to locate and educate yourself on additional oper.s that are available to you.

Chapter 5: Quotes and Strings

String values are included in the majority of PS illustrations. These are typically passed along to commands in the form of arguments. You will sometimes see that the strings are enclosed in single quotes, and other times you will see that they are instead enclosed in double quotes. Occasionally you will see that quotes do not enclose them at all. It is paramount for you to understand how to handle these strings properly. In order to ensure that you can do this, we will go over quoting rules, which are used to govern how strings are to be handled. You will learn the instances in which you are supposed to enclose string values in quotes, and you will even learn when to use single versus double quotes.

String Values

It is paramount to know that any time you place quotes around a text, PS will handle that as though it is a string value. With this in mind, as long as the text does not contain any reference scalers or special characters you can enclose text with either single or double quotes. You will learn more about special characters later in this chapter, and you will learn more about reference scalers in chapter 6. As far as enclosing text in quotes without either of those, you can see that the following illustrations will return the same results.

Write-Output "String in quotes."
 Write-Output 'String in quotes.'

In illustrations that are similar to the illustrations above, the **Write-Output** command directs a string object to the next command in the pipeline. In this specific example, the output is sent straight to the PS console. Upon running both of these commands you will see that the returned values are the same.

Similar to the **Write-Output** command, the **Out-Host** and the **Write-Host** commands in PS will output data directly to the console. The details of each are what makes them different. The **Write-Output** command will send the output down the line to command that is next in line. If it is the final command in the pipeline, then it will output the information directly to the console. The **Out-Host** command will also send it's output directly to the console, however, it offers an additional and optional parameter. This parameter will allow you to go through the output one screen at a time. This can be beneficial if there is a large amount of data being output. If a output command is not specified, then the process will default to **Out-Host.** Just like the previous two, the **Write-Host** command will output its data straight to the console. The difference with **Write-Host** lies in its customization potential. There are two additional parameters that allow you to change both the background and text.

If you are using basic quoted string values that are being directed to the console window, then you will see that all three of the commands behave in very similar ways. All four of the following illustrations will produce the same results.

"String in quotes."
 Write-Output "String in quotes."
 Write-Host "String in quotes."
 Out-Host `

-InputObject "String in quotes."

Because there is no command specified for the first illustration, it will automatically default to the **Out-Host** command.

It is paramount to remember that each of these output commands will respond differently to different situations. Because of this, it is advised that you check out each one's help file.
If you choose to use quotes within a string, you can use either single within double quotes, or double within double quotes, like the following:

Write-Output "String 'in' quotes."
 Write-Output 'String "in" quotes.'

You will see in the output that the inside quotes for each illustration will be carried through to the output. If you use identical quotes throughout the illustrations, it will not work out the same way, like the following illustrations:

Write-Output "String "in" quotes."
 Write-Output 'String 'in' quotes.'

You will see that the results for these a very different from the first two illustrations. For the two illustrations, we just used you should notice that the quotes are not displayed. In addition to this, there is a new line. This occurs because PS is interpreting one string as multiple strings, which results in a line break. PS is interpreting String as the very first string, which provides a line break, and then the rest is interpreted as another, different string. It is possible to use double inside double quotes, but in order to do that, you will have to escape those inside quotes. You will learn how to do that later in this book.

Anytime you are employing quotes it is paramount that you do not mix up the quote types. It is also a good idea to double check and make sure you don't forget one. If you do, it is possible for you to get trapped in a loop. In this situation, it will continually prompt you for entry, and no matter what you enter, it will not pull you out of the loop. If this happens to you, simply use Ctrl+C in order to return to your command prompt.

Write-Output "123"

Executing this illustration will return a value that is a string object. You can always verify the value's type with the following illustration:

(Write-Output "123").GetType()
The above illustration utilized the **GetType** method of accessing an object's type. In this case, the type is a System.String. We will go over this more shortly.

It is also paramount to observe that if you do not enclose a numerical value with quotes then PS will handle it as a numerical object, as shown in the following illustration:

Write-Output 123

Remember, you can always verify the object type by utilizing the **GetType** method, like the following illustration:

(Write-Output 123).GetType()

After running this illustration you will see that the object type is Int32. observe at this point that if a value includes both letters and numbers then PS will handle it as a string whether or not it is enclosed in quotes. If you run the following two illustrations you will see that the first will return a string. You can then verify this by running the second illustration.

Write-Output 123output
(Write-Output 123output).GetType()

If your argument is a string that has no spaces within it, then you can usually leave off the quotes. Running the next three illustrations that utilize the **Set-locale** command will set the operating folder to C drive:

Set-locale C:
Set-locale "C:\"
Set-locale 'C:\'

If you wish to instead change the operating folder to the C:\Documents and Settings folder, use the following illustration:

Set-locale `
C:\Documents and Settings

This will generate an error. This is because the illustration doesn't know how to utilize the words, or tokens, after the first space. This is because "and" is being interpreted as a parameter. Because there is not a parameter by this name, the error is generated. This can easily be fixed by putting quotes around the entire argument, like this:

Set-locale `
 "C:\Documents and Settings"

Once this illustration is run, the operating folder will change. Another thing to acknowledge when you are employing strings is how to properly reference scalers that are within quoted strings. If double-quotes are used to enclose the string, then the scaler's value will be used. If single quotes are used, then the literal value will be used. The next chapter will cover how to properly reference scalers. It wouldn't hurt to get a head start by utilizing the help files at **about_quoting_rules.**

Escaping Special Characters

So far, the examples that we have gone over were capable of taking on either single quotes or double quotes. You may not yet understand the difference between the two. You should acknowledge that there is a very paramount distinction. Single quotes will always handle a string quite literally. Double quotes, on the other hand, will allow you to escape the special characters that are in the text. The special character, when preceded by the backtick, or `, will take on specific actions that otherwise would not be accomplished without the presence of the backtick. Here is a list of PS's special characters (next page):

Special Character	Description
`0	Inserts a Null value
`a	Sends an alert (bell or beep) to the computer's speaker
`b	Inserts a backspace
`f	Inserts a form feed
`n	Inserts a new line
`r	Inserts a carriage return
`t	Inserts a horizontal tab
`v	Inserts a vertical tab
`'	Inserts a single quote
`"	Inserts a double quote

The quickest way for you to grasp this concept will be through seeing it in action. The next illustration is one in which several characters have been escaped. This is done in order to change how the text will be displayed.

Write-Output ("`n`tText includes" + ` "`n`t"escaped`" characters.`n")

As you can see, the first character to be escaped is **n**. You can tell this because it is the first letter to be preceded by the backtick. The letter n used in this manner will result in a new line. Next is the letter **t**, which results in a tab being inserted. Notice that the backtick that is used at the end of the first line is not being utilized for an escape character. It is, however, being used as a continuation character, indicating that the illustration continues into the next line. You should also observe the letter **n** appears twice more in the second line and the letter **t** appears once more. In addition to this, the double quotes around the word **escaped** are preceded by a backtick. This results in double quotes appearing in the output. Don't forget about those help files. You can find a lot more information on escaping characters via **about_escape_character**.

Now, if we try to escape characters within a string that are enclosed in single quotes, the special characters, and the backticks will have no effect on the resulting output other than the fact that they will be handled literally. Here is an example:

Write-Output '`tindented`n`twords'

This ends up returning the exact string as it was originally typed. It is paramount to know that pre-released versions of PS allowed you to escape characters from within single quoted strings. Remember that this was only for pre-released versions.

System.String Object Members

All strings within PS are handled as System.String objects. This provides more methods and properties that you can utilize. As mentioned previously, the **Get-Member** command is used to retrieve an object's members as it is passed along a pipeline. Since a string is also passed along as an object, you can utilize **Get-Member** for that string. Here is an example illustration:

"test output" | Get-Member

By running this illustration you will see that a string object can support numerous methods. These include GetType and Substring. By scrolling down, you will also see the length property. This property will tell you the number of characters that exist within that string. So let's say that we wish to know more about that Substring method that we mentioned. We can utilize the **Get-Member** to retrieve the desired information by using the following illustration:

"test output" |
Get-Member Substring |
Format-List

After running this illustration, you should observe that there are details indicating how to properly utilize this method.
There are two approaches to choose from when calling this method:

System.String Substring(Int32 startIndex)
 System.String Substring(Int32 startIndex, Int32 length)

In option one, you will be providing a target string as well as an integer. This integer is used to specify the position at which the substring will start. This will cause a return of a substring that begins at the desired position and continues to the end of that string. Here is an example illustration using **test output** and starting the substring at position 5:

("test output").Substring(5)

acknowledge that you have to enclose the target string with parentheses, and then you have to add a period after the method name. Additionally, the parameter must be enclosed in parentheses.

For the second option, you will provide the target string as well as the substring's starting point and length. Here is an example illustration of a substring beginning at the start of the string, or position 0, and that the substring will be four characters long:

("test output").Substring(0,4)

Calling a method such as GetType and Substring, they will generate their own object that will be directed down the pipeline. Because of this, you can still utilize the **GetMember** command to retrieve the object members. The next illustration will return a list of properties that are available to the **System.RuntimeType** object:

("test output").GetType() |
 Get-Member -MemberType Property

As you can see, the string will first be enclosed in parentheses, with a period following. Then you will have the method name, in this example it is **GetType**. The object is then directed down the line to **Get-Member**. For this example, we utilized the **-MemberType** parameter in order to display the object's properties.

Chapter Summary

As you have learned, most of the time string values play a vital role in many PS illustrations. With a deeper understanding of the use of strings, you will see the effectiveness of your illustrations increase. It is highly recommended and encouraged that you spend plenty of time practicing a variety of used with string in your illustrations. Practice with both single and double quotes. You should practice escaping those special characters as well. And as always, don't forget those help files in order to assist you to reach a better understanding of what you are using.

Chapter 6: scalers

scalers are best described as virtual duffel bags that are utilized in order to store and transport data within your PS code. You will find that some of these duffel bags come prepackaged for your convenience. The scalers that are built into both PS's and Windows environments come with data already allocated to them. You will also find instances in which you need user defined scalers, which you have to pack yourself. These take more work to use versus the built-in scalers, but they will contain everything that you need and can, therefore, be more beneficial. But we are getting ahead of ourselves. Before being capable of utilizing built-in, user defined, or environmental scalers, we will first have to get a grasp of the basics.

scalers: Built-In

There are several built-in scalers that are supported by PS. These provide different kinds of information, including the current operating folder, or $PWD, and the PS home folder, or $PSHOME. If you wish to access a complete list of scalers, including user defined scalers, that are available to you during the current running session, you can utilize the following illustration:

dir scaler: | sort name

We start this illustration of by utilizing the **Get-ChildItem** command alias, **dir.** This takes the **scaler** as its argument. This argument refers directly to the scaler drive, which is one of several drives that are supported by PS. We will go into greater detail on the topic of drives in the next chapter. As expected, this drive will provide you access to the PS scalers and their values, including both user defined and built-in scalers.

Once the **Get-ChildItem** command succeeds in retrieving the scalers and their associated values, they will be directed down the pipeline to the **SortObject** command. We utilized the alias, **sort**, for this illustration. This command will then sort the output data by the scalers' names. If you do not decide to sort the returned information by name, they will instead be displayed in their retrieved order.

This list of scalers that will be displayed can be extremely valuable to you as long as you keep one thing in mind. When referencing built in and user defined scalers within PS code, you will normally need to precede the name of the scaler with the $. This list may not include the dollar sign with their names, so you will have to remember to include it in your illustrations. This dollar sign is used in order to make scalers easier to distinguish from other elements of code. For instance, it can be rather easy to confuse the pwd alias and the $PWD scaler, which is built in. Having the money sign there helps you to more easily distinguish the difference in the two. You will come across a few instances in which the scaler does not require the dollar sign. We will discuss that later. Let's turn to an example.

If you are wishing to retrieve the value of one of the built-in scalers, all you have to do is enter the name of the scaler, including the dollar sign, like this:

$pshome

By running this illustration, you will have returned a path to the PS home folder. You can use any scaler, including built-in scalers, in illustrations. If you wish to retrieve a complete list of .dll files that from within the PS home folder, you can use the following illustration:

dir $pshome -filter *.dll

There are two separate types of built-in scalers that are supported by PS. These are automatic, like with $PSHOME, and preference, like with $MaximumErrorCount. The values for preference scalers are capable of being modified, however you cannot do this for automatic scalers. Trying to change the value of an automatic scaler will return an error. You can utilize the **about_preference_scalers** help files for a full list of current preference scalers available to you. On the other hand, by utilizing **about_automatic_scaler** help files for a full list of current automatic scalers that are accessible for your use.

In order to modify a preference scaler's value, you just have to use the assignment oper. to adjust the value. The assignment oper. is = . The preference scaler $MaximumErrorCount is used in order to specify the depth of the error history log in your current session. If you update or change the value, it will persist until it is either changed or you end your current session. If you wish to increase the value of the scaler from 256, which is the default, to 265, you can utilize this illustration:

$maximumerrorcount = 260

scalers: Environment

You can use the Env drive with PS in order to gain access to the Windows environment scalers. If you wish to return a complete list of the Windows environment scalers, as well as their values, you can utilize the following illustration to access that list and sort them by their names:

dir env: | sort name

Similar to both user-defined scalers and built-in scalers, the list of environment scalers does not include the required prefix that is needed to be included within in PS code when referencing those scalers. However, it is paramount to know that there is a difference in the prefixes used for environment scalers, as compared to the previously discussed scalers. In the user defined scalers and built in scalers we utilized the money sign, $, as a prefix. With the environmental scalers we will have to use $env at the beginning of the environment scaler's name whenever we reference it. If we wish to retrieve the value of the windir environment scaler, we can utilize the following illustration:

$env:windir

In order to receive a complete list of all .dll files located in the Windows home folder, we would use:

dir $env:windir -filter *.dll

It is also good to know that you can change the values of each of the environment scalers. Let's say that you wish to modify the value of the HOMEPATH environment scaler from \Documents and Settings\administrator, and have instead be \Documents and Settings\administrator\home. In order to accomplish this you can utilize the + oper. in order to add the string \home to the value of the HOMEPATH environments scaler, as follows:

$env:homepath =
 $env:homepath + "\home"

Just like with the previous $MaximumErrorCount scaler, this change will persist until it is either changed again, or you end the current session.

scalers: List-Defined

Some scripting languages require that you explicitly state a scaler prior to its use. Fortunately, PS does not restrict you in this manner. All you have to do is assign the scaler a value. For instance, processing the following illustration will assign the string one-two to the scaler $var1:

$var1 = "one two"

By defining a scaler in this manner, you are in fact calling the **New-scaler** command. This ends up providing two arguments to it, which are the value and name of the scaler. For example, to achieve the same results as the last illustration, we can utilize this illustration:

New-scaler var1 "one two"

You have surely noticed that the scaler's name in this illustration did not have a dollar sign at the front of it. There are specific situations in which you do not have to utilize the dollar sign. Such situations include any time that the scaler's name is part of the argument to the **New-scaler** command, **Clear-scaler** command, **Set-scaler** command, **or the Removescaler** command.

There is an additional benefit to utilizing the **New-scaler** command. Using it to create a new scaler allows you to take advantage of other command parameters. For instance, you can utilize the **-option** parameter in order to set a read-only definition to the scaler, like the following illustration:

New-scaler var1 "one two" `
-option ReadOnly

As you can see here, we have specified **ReadOnly** as the **-option** parameter's argument. In addition to this, you can also specify other values as arguments in this parameter. All you have to do is to be sure that you separate each argument with a comma. You can utilize the **New-scaler** help file in order to access a complete list of available and acceptable arguments. By setting a scaler to read only, you are making it so that the value of the scaler cannot be changed unless the change is forced. Let's look at how we change or update a scaler first. The easiest way to change the value of a scaler is by utilizing the = oper., like this:

$var1 = "three"

By utilizing the **Set-scaler** command you can accomplish the same returns, like this:

Set-scaler var1 "three"

These illustrations will both reset the value of the scaler, but this is only if the scaler has not previously been defined as read-only. If the scaler had been sent to read only, you will only return an error without updating its value. The way to circumvent this would be to force the change by invoking the -**force** parameter, like we have done here:

Set-scaler var1 "three" -force

This will assign a new value to the scaler. Much like the **New-scaler** command, you can use additional parameters with the **Set-scaler** command. You can also clear the value of one of these scalers. One way to do so is to set the value of the scaler to null. You can do this using the built-in scaler $null, like this:

$var1 = $null

Alternately, you can achieve the same result by using the **Clear-scaler** command, as in the following illustration:
Clear-scaler var1

Just as we described before, if this scaler is set has read only, then each of the commands will fail. In order to get around this, you will need to force it just like before. Here is how you force the previous illustration:

Clear-scaler var1 `
 -force

It is also possible to completely delete a scaler. If you wish to delete a scaler, you can do so by using the **Remove-scaler** command, as follows:

Remove-scaler var1

Again, if the scaler is set to be ready only, it will only return a scaler. As I am sure you can deduce, there is a way to get around this, and that is to force it, using the **-force** parameter as follows:

Remove-scaler var1 -force

Most of the time it is much easier to just use the = oper. in order to adjust scalers, allowing you to change, clear, or create scalers. Alternately, if you decide you wish to use the **New-scaler, Set-scaler, Clear-scaler,** or **Remove-scaler** commands, and wish to learn more about them, you can retrieve their associated help files.

Other Types of Data

Here we are going to look into other things that you should consider when approaching user defined scalers. To get started, first, you will need to create $var1. Do so with the following illustration:

$var1 = "one two"

You needed to recreate this because we recently deleted it with the **Remove-scaler** command. As previously mentioned with the built in scaler values, you can also retrieve the values of user-defined scalers by just by entering the scalers name. Do not forget the money sign.

$var1

We assigned a string value to **$var1** when we ran **$var1 = "one two".** Because of this, PS has stored the value as a string object. Remember, you can always verify an object type by utilizing the **GetType()** method, just like this:

$var1.gettype()

It is also good to know that when you are creating a scaler you are not limited to just string values. For example, you can assign an integer to the scaler value quite easily, as follows:

$var1 = 123; $var1.gettype()

By running the above illustration, PS will automatically store the value and do so using the correct type, which in this case is Int32. After running this illustration, you will see multiple illustrations returned. If you wish to manually terminate the illustration then you can use the semicolon. Knowing this, you can run multiple illustrations in one line, as long as they are separated by a semicolon.

You can also assign values other than strings or integers when creating a scaler. The process is exactly the same, as follows:

$var1 = 12.34; $var1.gettype()

$var1 = get-date; $var1.gettype()

The first illustration is used to store the value type as **Double**. The second illustration is used to store the value type as **GetDate.**

Now let's say that you wish to append text to an already existing string value within a user defined scaler. You can follow the same approach that we utilized for adding the text to an existing string in the environmental scalers. Let's say we wish to append a string to **$var1**, we can do the following:

$var1 = "one two three"; $var1
$var1 = $var1 + " four"; $var1

As you can see, we have appended the string four to this after assigning a string value.

You can do an operation that is similar by utilizing numerical values, just like the following illustration:

$var1 = 123; $var1
$var1 = $var1 + 4; $var1

The results for the previous illustration will be different, but why? That is because we did not use quotes in the illustration. Instead of appending the number 4, PS actually just adds 4 to the total amount. Instead, runt the illustration like this:

$var1 = "123"; $var1

$var1 = $var1 + 4; $var1

Now, by properly utilizing our quotes, the number 4 will be appended to the original. You can utilize this process with any string, just like this:

$var1 = "one two three"; $var1
 $var1 = $var1 + 4; $var1

The results returned might seem a bit peculiar, but PS has done exactly what you told it to do.
Even though you have the ability to append a number or text to a string, the opposite is not true. If you try to append a string, let's take string four, to the number 123, you will receive an error. Here is that illustration:

$var1 = 123; $var1
 $var1 = $var1 + "four"; $var1

You are only capable of appending a value to another, pre-existing value if both of the values are compatible with each other. PS will try to do what you wish and let you assign any type of data to scalers as long as what you assign can be converted into the correct data type.

scalers: Referencing Within Strings

It is possible to use scalers within strings in PS. It is paramount to acknowledge, however, that the way scalers are handled at runtime will depend on your usage of either single or double quotes. With single quotes, PS will output the scaler's name as it was entered. With double quotes, PS will instead output the value of the scaler. For instance, we will assign the string scaler that is named **$svc** the value of **eventlog** in the following illustration:

$svc = "eventlog"

Now that we have that completed we can utilize the scaler in our strings. All we have to do is type out the name of the scaler just as we would with any other word, just like this:

Write-Output "The service is $svc."
Even though we use the dollar sign, which indicates to PS that the word is a scaler, because it is enclosed in the double quotes PS will replace the name of the scaler with the value of the scaler. This ends up with the result: The service is eventlog. So what happens when we use single quotes, like the following:

Write-Output 'The service is $svc.'

Because of the use of single quotes, the scaler will be handled as though it is a literal value. This will cause PS to output the name of the scaler, which will result in: The service is $svc. Let's say that you wish to do a combination of the two, including both the name of the scaler as well as its value in a string. In order to accomplish this, you will need to use double quotes and then the backtick in order to escape the scaler that you wish kept as literal. This is shown in the following example:

Write-Output `

"The value of `$svc is $svc."

Again, it is paramount to understand that the backtick being used at the end of the first line is not being utilized to escape a character, but rather it is being used in order to continue the illustration. The illustration results in: The value of $svc is eventlog. What happens if we use single quotes again?

Write-Output `
'The value of `$svc is $svc.'

This illustration will result in the PS outputting the string as it is entered, including the backtick, resulting in: The value of `$svc is $svc.

PS outputs the string as it's entered, backtick and all: The value of `$svc is $svc.

scalers: As Arguments

So far you have learned how to include a scaler in a string value that is passed along to the **Write-Output** command as an argument. There will be instances in which you will wish to utilize a scaler as an argument for a command without including it in a string. When you come across these circumstances you can simply use that scaler as your argument. As an example, the following illustration employs the $svc scaler as the argument for the **Get-Service** command. Look at the following illustration:

Get-Service "$svc"

This will return the same results. The reason for this, as you have already seen, PS will receive the value of the scaler when double quotes enclose it. You have also seen what happens when we use single quotes rather than double quotes. PS interprets the name of the scaler literally. Like in the following illustration:

Get-Service '$svc'

This illustration will fail. This is because PS interprets the name of the service as '$svc'.

Chapter summary

As you have seen throughout this chapter, scalers are vital when you are looking for effective scripting. This is the same for user defined scalers, built in scalers, as well as environment scalers. If properly utilized, you will soon find that these are very valuable tools for you to use in scripts and on the command line. Remember to go over the PS help files for information on each of the scalers. It would be a great idea to take the time to practice with those scalers, both creating, modifying, and utilizing each kind. You will soon see that as you progress into more complex coding that scalers will begin to appear more and more.

Chapter 7: Drives and Providers

When using PS, you will gain access to different folders and files by first providing an appropriate path name. An example of a path name is C:\Windows\System32. The pathname for this example begins with C. That is the name of the drive. Whenever you are attempting to access a specific file system resource, you will first have to provide PS with the name of the drive. Either that or the drive will have to be implied within the command's context. That means, for instance, that if you wish to have a list of information returned to you from the current workstation, you will not have to specify the drive.

There are drives other than file system drives that are supported by PS. PS does, in fact, support a number of different drives that will provide you with access to many different data stores. An example of one is the scaler drive that we mentioned earlier in the book. This drive is used to provide you access to the available built-in scalers. We also partially went off the Env drive, which we mentioned is used to provide access to the available environment scalers.

In our final chapter of PS: The Ultimate Beginner's Guide, we will teach you all about the available drives, as well as the different ways to utilize them through PS providers that enable access to different data stores. You will also learn about the built-in drives within PS, as well as how to create whole new drives. By the time you reach the end of this chapter, you will understand how to go about accessing the file system, the registry, the certificate store, as well as other data stores.

PS Providers

It is paramount to understand that the core of data store access resides within PS providers. One such provider is Microsoft .NET. This is a program, which provides you with a data access layer. This layer is between the data and PS itself. This layer, and by relation the providers, allow you to connect with various data stores by utilizing different PS mechanisms. For instance, it is possible for you to employ the **Get-Children** command in order to access the file system, registry, and the certificate data stores.

There are many providers that are built into PS. In order to view a complete list of the currently available providers on your system, you should run the following illustration:

Get-PSProvider | select Name

There is potential for a vast variety of providers to become available to you. This is because PS is extensible. You can locate many providers and install them in order to provide you with different data stores. These are referred to as customer providers.

Below is a list of currently built-in providers that are shipped along with PS.

Provider	Data Store
Alias	PS built-in and user-defined aliases
Certificate	Windows digital signature certificates
Environment	Windows environment scalers
FileSystem	Windows file system drives, folders, and files
Function	PS functions
Registry	Windows registry
scaler	PS scalers

Even though providers are a vital part of the coding process, they are basically invisible to you when within PS. On the other hand, you can see the PS drives that are used in order to access these providers.

Drives: Built In

PS drives are utilized in order to return the data from providers. For instance, file system data from the file system provider is exposed via the PS drives that directly corresponds with your system's Windows drives. The PS C drive, for example, access data via the file system provider, which will expose your system's Windows C drive. To view a full list of PS drives and their providers, use the following illustration:

Get-PSDrive | sort Provider, Name

Using this illustration will sort by provider first, and then by name. This will result in providers being grouped together. You will see how many drives are supported by each provider. This illustration will also display the root information. This information is used to locate the target data store, which the PS drive maps to. For instance, the **HKEY_CURRENT_USER** hive is mapped to by the HKCU drive. The root value will be blank for instances in which the drives access nonhierarchical data, like with aliases and scalers.

For more information on specific drives, you can utilize the **Get-PSDrive** command. For example, if we wish information on the function drive:

Get-PSDrive Function | Format-List

This will return details on the drive as well as the provider. It will also show the following illustration:

Get-PSDrive -PSProvider Registry

This returns a list of all drives that are associated with the provider titled **Registry.** Once you find out the available drives, you can use your commands and illustrations to access them. Like with the following, which is used in order to change the operating locale to the Env drive:

cd Env:\

Here we used the **Set-locale** alias of **cd**. You will then see that the locale has been changed. Once in this folder, you can utilize PS commands, like this:

dir | where {$_.Name -like "*path*"}

Here we used the **Get-Children** alias of **dir**. Then we filtered out scaler names that did not meet the specified criteria. It works the same way as it would within the file system drive. It is possible to access any drive type from within any other drive type, like the following:

dir HKCU:

The above illustration will retrieve a list of all of the objects that are in the HKCU drive, and does so without altering the operating locale. It is also possible to change from one drive type to any other, like the following:

cd HKCU:\Software\Microsoft\Office

This illustration changed our operating locale to the registry key. On top of all of this, you can also change over to differ folders within drives in any hierarchical data store. It also does not make a difference if you access data via different providers or not, like in the following illustration, which access registry key information from a different hive:

dir HKLM:\Software\Microsoft\Office

A benefit of using drives in PS is that you are capable of jumping to multiple locales without any special steps being required. If you wish to access information about an item, like the registry key, or the **HKEY_LOCAL_MACHINE\Software Microsoft\ASP.NET**, you can use the following:

```
Get-ItemProperty `
 HKLM:\Software\Microsoft\ASP.NET
```

That illustration will retrieve a list of the properties, their values, as well as information specific to PS, like the PS drive name and provider. Additionally, the built-in drives for PS can be used to take different actions that are applicable to each data store. You can use the following to create a new object within the registry:

```
New-Item `
 HKLM:\Software\Microsoft\TestKey1
```

This will add the **TestKey1** Object into the **HKEY_LOCAL_MACHINE\Software\Microsoft**. Once this has been done, you can add a property to the key, such as **TestProperty**, by using the following command:

```
New-ItemProperty `
 HKLM:\Software\Microsoft\TestKey1 `
 -Name TestProperty -PropertyType string `
 -Value "test value"
```

This new property has test value as its value. This data type is a string data type. After running the illustration, PS will return information on all properties and values, including the new property. There are other actions that can be taken via the PS drives, like using the **Rename-Item** command to rename **TestKey1** to **TestKey2**, as follows:

```
Rename-Item `
 HKLM:\Software\Microsoft\TestKey1 `
 TestKey2
```

The first argument in this command is used to identify the original key, **TestKey1**, and the second argument is used to provide the new name, **TestKey2**. Additionally, you can remove the registry key via the **Remove-Item** command, like this:

Remove-Item `
 HKLM:\Software\Microsoft\TestKey2

As you can see with the use of the previous illustrations, operating in other drives is very similar to employing the file system drive. On top of what you have already learned, you can also utilize the same commands with other files and folders, as well as their contents.

Drives: Create

So far you have only seen how to use built in PS drives. Now you will learn how to create your own drives that are based on existing providers. This is especially beneficial for simplifying your commands and illustrations. In order to create a new drive for PS, we will first need to use the **New-PSDrive** command, like we did below for the drive named **ps.**

New-PSDrive -Name ps `
 -PSProvider FileSystem -Root $pshome

This illustration first identifies the name of the new drive. Afterward it names the provider, and finally, it names the root.

When running this illustration, PS will create the drive and then display the information about that drive. You will notice that the information displayed is actually the root name, and not the scaler name. Once the drive has been created, you can then utilize it in the same fashion as the built in drives. If you wished to change your operating locale to the newly created drive, you could use this illustration:

cd ps:

Once this is done, you will be capable of working in the new drive. You may come across instances in which you are not sure if you are operating in the proper folder. In order to check that, you can utilize the **Get-ChildItem** command. You will notice in the results that the name of the operating locale is displayed.

You are also capable of deleting or removing user created or user defined drives via the use of the **Remove-PSDrive** command. It is paramount to observe that you cannot be operating in the drive that you are wishing to delete, so you may have to change your operating locale. Once you have done that, use the following illustration:

cd C:\\; Remove-PSDrive ps

It is also paramount to know that the drives that you create in a session will only persist through that session. You will not have to go through the process of removing or deleting the drive, unless, of course, you have an explicit reason to do so. You might wish to do this in order to simplify the list of drives available to you when you are done using a specific drive. You can only have user defined drives persist across multiple session by altering your profile file.

Chapter Summary

In the final chapter of this book, you learned how PS drives are utilized, what PS providers are, as well as how to create your own user-defined drives. Remember to use your help files in order to access more information on anything that you need. Also, don't forget to practice everything that you have learned. After all, a new language will never stick without practice!

Conclusion

Thank you again for purchasing this book!

I hope this book was capable of helping you to learn the basics of programming and scripting with PS.

The next step is to practice what you have learned and use your help files to further your understanding of each aspect of PS.

Finally, if you found this book useful, then I'd like to ask you for a favor, would you be kind enough to leave a review for this book on Amazon? It'd be greatly appreciated!

Thank you and good luck!

Other Books by Timothy Short

Linux: The Quick Start Beginners Guide

Wordpress: Beginner to Pro Guide

Shopify: Beginner to Pro Guide

Passive Income: The Ultimate Guide to Financial Freedom

Project Management: Beginner to Professional Manager and Respected Leader

Blockchain: The Comprehensive Guide to Mastering the Hidden Economy

Raspberry Pi 3: Beginner to Pro Guide

Evernote: Made Simple: Master Time Management and Productivity

All available via amazon.com

42163408R00051

Made in the USA
San Bernardino, CA
28 November 2016